WHAT PEOPLE AR

SOUL CO.

In a society... where spirituality is too often neglected or at best misunderstood as religion, comes along a book that firmly places spirituality, consciousness and the meaning of life and death in the forefront of its considerations. As someone who has both journeyed with dying and grieving people and experienced my own major losses, I can honestly convey my sense of being so moved by *Soul Comfort*. For its poetry and flow, for its digestible, bite-sized reflections, and for the sincerity and wisdom held within its pages, this book offers its reader an opportunity to explore the depths and heights of our Being-ness.

Dr. Monika Wilson, psychotherapist, teacher and founder of ReConnections Counselling Service

In *Soul Comfort*, Alistair Conwell provides light to those who see only darkness, as he recognizes what he describes as the "dance between the heart and the soul"... Those who are fortunate to read *Soul Comfort* will undoubtedly replace fear with understanding as they continue on their soul's journey.

Bob Ginsberg, Co-founder, Forever Family Foundation

Alistair offers a comforting approach to those dealing with grief in this beautiful profound book that focuses on the soul to soul, heart to heart connections that go so far beyond this physical universe. *Soul Comfort* reminds us that consciousness transcends all, including the death of the physical body, and that a grieving heart truly is a loving soul...

Andrea R. Garrison, author of *The Crossing Over of Mattie Pearl* and Host/Producer of Online with Andrea

This book will be so affirming to those who already realize that the soul connections we have with loved ones are not severed by death. And, it will be eye opening for those people who are just realizing that the... nonphysical is our natural state of being.

Conwell contends that exploring the subjects of life and death can provide the ultimate transformational, personal experience, if we are open to it. *Soul Comfort* is affirming and calming. I have added it to my recommended reading list for anyone creating the next chapter of life... after loss.

Lynne McCollum Staley, Grief Recovery Specialist, Life After Loss Coach, and author of *In Death is the Secret to Life*

This lovely book is one that can be read over and over again and new insights will arise with each reading. Death and grief are things that will come to us all so this book could be of great help to each one of us at some point in our lives. It offers a deeply spiritual perspective of death, and consequently, life. Read this book often, very slowly and with an open mind, and it could give you a completely different understanding of both life and death.

Dr. Penny Sartori, author of *The Wisdom of Near-Death Experiences*

A profound and poetic articulation of the nature of soul, consciousness and the spiritual connections we share with loved ones in this life and beyond. It should provide much comfort to those grieving a loss.

Miriam Knight, Publisher and Editor, *New Consciousness Review*

Soul Comfort

Uplifting Insights into the Nature of
Grief, Death, Consciousness and
Love for Transformation

Soul Comfort

Uplifting Insights into the Nature of
Grief, Death, Consciousness and
Love for Transformation

Alistair Conwell

BOOKS

Winchester, UK
Washington, USA

First published by O-Books, 2016
O-Books is an imprint of John Hunt Publishing Ltd., Laurel House, Station Approach,
Alresford, Hants, SO24 9JH, UK
office1@jhpbooks.net
www.johnhuntpublishing.com

For distributor details and how to order please visit the 'Ordering' section on our website.

ISBN: 978 1 78535 173 0
Library of Congress Control Number: 2015943105

A CIP catalogue record for this book is available from the British Library.

Design: Lee Nash

Printed and bound by CPI Group (UK) Ltd, Croydon, CR0 4YY, UK

We operate a distinctive and ethical publishing philosophy in all
areas of our business, from our global network of authors to
production and worldwide distribution.

CONTENTS

For
Mum, Pop and Sarah

Acknowledgments

I must extend my sincere gratitude to Sarah Neale, who kindly read the first drafts of this book and whose feedback significantly shaped its format. Thank you, Sarah, for also asking the correct questions.

Look well into thyself. There is a source of strength which will always spring up if thou will always look there.
~ Marcus Aurelius (121–180)

He that conceals his grief finds no remedy for it.
~ Turkish Proverb

Though lovers be lost, love shall not; And death shall have no dominion.
~ Dylan Thomas (1914–1953)

Preface

Most people believe that death and taxes are the only certainties in life. But there is a third certainty – grief. Grief is equally certain because it always follows the death of a loved one's physical body and will even begin if you know that their death, or indeed the death of your own body, is imminent as a result of age, illness or a traumatic event.

Grief is a normal, instinctive emotional response to loss or impending loss. Every day we experience a range of emotions depending on what events occur in our lives. In life's emotional and spiritual journey, there is indeed a deceptively fine line between pleasure and pain. For love is the pleasure of souls and grief is the pain of love.

Grief is a complex emotion that changes whoever it touches. The changes can be profound or quite subtle, conscious or unconscious, rapid or slow yet the experience of grief changes you or at the very least begins a change process. Embracing the change is key for your healing and positive transformation.

Whether or not the death of your loved one's physical body occurs unexpectedly, there is always a sense of disbelief and shock (and a range of other emotions) when the death actually occurs. Each of us will grieve differently as we process and try to deal with all the everyday implications of the loss. To find that someone deeply loved is no longer physically present is difficult, indeed some of us may find impossible, to accept. You may have thoughts that your loved one will physically present themselves at any moment. And you will yearn to just touch them and hold them in your arms again. You may feel that you lose a part of yourself or that there is a feeling of something missing – a gaping immeasurable Grand Canyon of emptiness, pushed into your life. There is always pain, sometimes it is physical, and there is always an indescribable sorrow. And you may wonder how others can go about their daily activities as if nothing has happened while your world has been shattered and seemingly stopped.

Although there is a widely-held view that achieving a 'sense of closure' or the passage of time extricates you from the grip of grief, mental health professionals are finding that for many people the grieving process never really ends no matter how much time passes or even if there is a 'sense of closure'. The grief you experience may change over time but that does not mean that the grieving process necessarily ceases.

The grieving process is like being alone in a vast ocean. You will find there are places in that ocean where it is so deep that it cannot be plumbed while elsewhere there are shallows. In some places, there are high surging swells, and there are other places where the surface is calm and smooth. Some days you will find yourself wading in calm shallow waters and on other days struggling in deep rough seas. But each of us has the natural ability to float, and no matter where in that vast ocean of grief you find yourself, take comfort knowing that the arms of the soul will not allow you to sink below the water's surface.

It is important to seek support from family and friends and, if necessary, mental health professionals when you are grieving. Yet seeking help when you are struggling with grief may be difficult at times because grief saps your self-confidence and courage, and at different times it can leave you feeling confused, guilty, isolated, angry, wounded, fearful, fragile and vulnerable. But what you may not realize is that your grief and all the associated feelings are the love pangs of your soul, because a grieving heart is a reflection of a loving soul. For that reason, the fragility and vulnerability you may feel are not weaknesses but are deemed strengths in the eyes of the soul.

A belief in a universal spiritual being like God, Allah, Brahma, the Tao or Elohim and so on (a sense of the spiritual is much more important than a cultural label) may assist some people during the grieving process or it may lead others to question their belief systems. Questions are useful even if answers may not seem readily forthcoming. A search for answers will inevitably lead to introspection or reflection, and this in itself can be a therapeutic process when you are grieving.

The ancient Greek edict, 'know thyself', is a clarion call for self-reflection and spiritual development. To 'know thyself' is to know the spirit within. Importantly, self-reflection should not be confused with the destructive narcissistic behaviors associated with *self-absorption* where someone is driven by selfishness and has an unrealistic and grossly inflated perception of themselves.

In contrast to self-absorption, positive and deep self-reflection requires peace and silence. Many people unconsciously fear silence and will engage in all sorts of distracting activities to avoid it. But there is no reason to fear silence. If you fear silence, you really fear being with yourself. Silence is not empty. Silence overflows with spirituality. Indeed, silence, reflection, love and humility are the most precious offerings on the sacred altar of the soul.

In reflecting on my own experiences of grief either directly or through those close to me, I found that common themes emerged beyond the concept of grief itself. I realized that the concepts of death, consciousness, love and transformation are each inherently linked to the concept of grief and to each other. The common theme is spirituality. So to better understand your grief and what you are experiencing, it is important to understand the nature of consciousness, death and love because that understanding will assist in your healing and positive spiritual transformation.

Importantly, your perception of grief and how you deal with it is framed by how you perceive death. For most of us, death is an uncomfortable mystery. So in Western societies in particular, there is a widespread fear of death. That fear is expressed consciously and hidden unconsciously. Most of us prefer not to discuss death, and those that do tend to couch it in euphemisms. But death is merely a portal through which consciousness passes unhindered by the physical body.

The death of the physical body does not extinguish consciousness. Instead, death transforms and distils consciousness by removing only the outermost layer of the ego, leaving a purified ego-consciousness with the memories and identity of your loved one intact. This means you remain spiritually connected with your loved one even after their physical body dies. Indeed, there are many higher and more subtle forms of ego-consciousness. Soul-consciousness is the highest and purest form of consciousness. The nature of the deathless soul is consciousness, and the nature of consciousness is love. And the grief you feel for someone is proportionate to the love you feel for them – the deeper your love, the deeper your grief. Indeed, the power of grief comes from the power of love.

If you are able to see death in a spiritual context then you must also see grief in the same way. By acknowledging the sense of the spiritual, you will be receptive to the possibility of positive spiritual transformation. That receptiveness is important because the spiritual transformation of consciousness is inevitable at the time of death – an event that awaits every one of us (remember it is one of the certainties of life). In that sense, your grief can be seen as a preparation for the death of your own physical body, whenever that will be.

The literature on near-death experiences alone provides compelling firsthand accounts, from thousands of people, of consciousness existing independently of the physical body. These amazing accounts come from the religious and nonreligious alike, so it cannot be argued that a belief in the continuation of consciousness after the demise of the physical body is merely blind religious faith or superstition not based on credible evidence.

In fact, scientific studies are also finding evidence of consciousness continuing after the death of the physical body. For instance, in 2014 a study sponsored by the University of Southampton in the United Kingdom found that hospital patients in different countries reported awareness of real events (not hallucinations) for a period after their hearts stopped beating, in one case for three minutes. This is significant because the brain ceases functioning only within 20 to 30 seconds of the heart stopping yet some patients were able to demonstrate a conscious awareness well beyond that point. And some patients in the study reported the typical characteristics of a near-death experience.

In my first book, *The Audible Life Stream: Ancient Secret of Dying While Living*, I devoted an entire chapter examining various theories that have been proposed over the years attempting to explain the near-death experience as something other than an experience of death itself. I concluded that none of the theories are viable, and suggest near-death experiences are named incorrectly because they are not experiences *near* death; they are actual experiences *of* death. In many cases, the experiences occurred in hospital settings during or following complications in medical procedures, and in some instances the patients were pronounced dead by doctors before they regained consciousness in their physical bodies.

While writing my first book, and after its publication, I spent significant time reflecting on death and those related concepts of consciousness, love, grief and transformation. So writing *Soul Comfort*, which is the first book to take a holistic view of grief, seemed perfectly logical and indeed necessary.

The purpose of this book is to make you pause and reflect after reading each page because a quiet, still and open mind is key to deepening your sense of the spiritual and initiating positive transformation. And it's within the context of that positive spiritual transformation where the potential for healing resides. Yet your journey of grief must be experienced in a way and at a pace with which you are comfortable. Grief cannot be rushed. The experience must be slowly processed. It is a milestone experience in life – a 'coming of age' in a spiritual sense. And it's not a case of integrating your grief into your life but more about integrating your life, through a trans-formative process, into your grief. But only you will know when you are past the initial shock, debilitating confusion and emotional turmoil of grief and at a point where you will be open to the potential for healing and transformation.

Therefore, these insights and reflections are deliberately presented concisely and clearly for a quiet, still and open mind. My sincere hope is that they will assist you to better understand your unique experience of grief by encouraging you to quietly reflect on your perceptions of it, and on the related concepts of death, consciousness, love and transfor-mation. In doing so, you will find you have embarked on a journey to better understand yourself – not just on an emotional level but on a deeper spiritual level too. If you do reflect and begin to question your perceptions, you can be certain that your journey of healing and positive spiritual transformation has commenced.

Alistair Conwell
25 May 2015

Consciousness

Consciousness is the inherent fabric of the universe

Like the invisible air our bodies share in the physical realm, consciousness is unseen yet all-pervasive. Consciousness is the multilevel fabric of the universe. The multiple levels of consciousness can be thought of as ascending floors in a skyscraper. Just as the view of a city would be limited from the ground floor of a 100-storey skyscraper, the view gets better and more expansive if you were to progressively ascend to higher floors. And if you were to go to the rooftop, the 360-degree panoramic bird's eye view would be spectacular. Not only would you see much more of the city, its surrounds and the skyline, you would also gain a completely new perspective of the city and perhaps see things you did not know even existed. So when your loved one's physical body dies, their awareness of the 'ground floor' of consciousness merely transitions to a higher 'storey', either closer to the rooftop or perhaps even to it.

Consciousness is the silent harmony of the universe

Consciousness is a spiritual vibration. As that vibration can have musical qualities, consciousness can be regarded as the silent harmony of the universe or the 'music of the spheres' that the ancient Greek philosopher and mathematician, Pythagoras, referred to. The stronger the spiritual connection between you and your loved one, the greater consciousness is shared at multiple levels of consciousness and the deeper the love between the two of you. That spiritual connection is made at higher levels of consciousness long before our physical lives.

The soul is an indestructible spiritual diamond unaffected by the demise of the physical body

The soul is inherently spiritual in its nature whereas the body is inherently physical. Consciousness enlivens the physical body but it can also exist independently of the physical body. In the same way that our modern technology requires electricity or Wi-Fi (wireless technology) to operate, the physical body requires consciousness to function. If a TV or mobile device malfunctions and becomes inoperable, that does not affect or eliminate the supply of electricity or Wi-Fi. Equally, the death of the physical body does not affect or eliminate consciousness – it simply transforms consciousness by raising its vibrational frequency to apprehend the spiritual realm.

We are not defined by our physical bodies but by our consciousness

The physical body is like a vehicle you may drive (including autonomous or self-drive vehicles that sense the environment automatically and need little more than a destination to be identified by the 'driver'). The vehicle enables you to use the road network and transports you to your destination, yet you are not defined by the vehicle. You have a separate identity to the vehicle. You can enter or exit from the vehicle at any time just as consciousness enters and exits the physical body. Although we identify ourselves with our physical bodies when alive, the physical body is merely the vehicle for which consciousness is the driver. Death is the process of consciousness exiting the physical body. That process is not painful; it is actually liberating and thrilling because any pain or discomfort experienced in the physical body prior to its death ceases, and the transition to the spiritual realm is usually associated with a feeling of travelling at rapid speed as the vibrational frequency of consciousness is raised.

Consciousness connects all beings – before and after death

In life and after death, each of us contributes soul-consciousness to the collective conscious soul of the universe – both its physical and spiritual aspects. Consciousness connects you and your loved one in the physical and spiritual realms. Just as countless water droplets collectively make up an enormous ocean, countless droplets of consciousness collectively make up the conscious soul of the universe. There is nowhere in the universe that is void of consciousness. Even inanimate objects are imbibed with consciousness but of an extremely low vibrational frequency. The nature of the soul is consciousness of the highest vibrational frequency.

The eternal light of consciousness cannot be dimmed by the dark clouds of death

Even on wintery days, the largest, darkest storm clouds cannot completely eliminate the light from the sun. Consciousness, like light, cannot be completely destroyed by the darkness of death. When your loved one's physical body dies, their consciousness is transitioned to an awareness of a spiritual reality. More subtle forms of their ego-consciousness remain at higher spiritual levels of consciousness. The layers of consciousness can be imagined to be like the anatomy of plant seeds. Just as seeds have an outer coat (called the testa) and multiple layers of endosperm that enclose the embryo, consciousness is also multilayered and at its core is the soul. Higher vibrational levels of consciousness are enclosed within the outermost level of ego-consciousness. There are numerous other higher vibrational levels of consciousness that each correspond to a spiritual reality. Each spiritual reality corresponds to a different level of conscious awareness. The death of your loved one's physical body takes their awareness to, or closer to, their core soul-consciousness as a result of the transitioning of their consciousness. But their consciousness is not destroyed. Therefore, your loved one will always remain connected with you spiritually and you with them, even when the physical connection is broken.

Death is the distiller not extinguisher of consciousness

Death does not extinguish consciousness. The death of the physical body actually distils or refines consciousness by dissolving the physical senses and removing only the outermost layer of ego-consciousness. Consciousness is distilled just like water is distilled through vaporization. In both cases it is a purification process. The higher forms of ego-consciousness retain memories and personality traits that characterize us as physical beings. So only a small aspect of your loved one's identity dies with their physical body. Each of us functions at all the higher levels of consciousness simultaneously; but for most of us, we can only be fully aware of the physical reality because our senses block out our awareness of the spiritual reality and higher levels of consciousness. Your dreams and intuition sometimes give you access to those higher spiritual levels of awareness where you interact with your loved one and other people you know regardless of whether their physical bodies are alive or dead.

Consciousness is shared on many levels

There are countless levels of consciousness between the outermost layer of ego-consciousness that inhabits the physical body and soul-consciousness. At each progressively higher level of consciousness there is greater awareness of the universe and a deeper sense of spirituality because awareness moves closer to soul-consciousness. Soul-consciousness equates to universal awareness of all levels of consciousness in the eternal present moment. However, most of us have full awareness of only one level of consciousness at any given time until awareness of soul-consciousness is achieved. You share consciousness with your loved one at many corresponding levels of consciousness and it does not matter if their physical body is alive or not.

The higher the level of consciousness, the deeper the love

The layer of ego-consciousness is strongest in the physical realm because it is created and sustained by our five senses. At each subsequent higher and distilled level of consciousness, the influence of the ego is diminished and the influence of the soul is enhanced. As soul-consciousness is the most unified form of consciousness, the inherent nature of the soul is love. So, the enhanced awareness at progressively higher levels of consciousness takes you to deeper levels of love. Therefore, the spiritual connection of consciousness and love between you and your loved one progressively deepens at higher levels of consciousness.

Consciousness connects you to someone not the physical body

The connection between you and your loved one remains unbroken after their physical body dies. Your memories, thoughts and, above all else, love connects you and your loved one as conscious beings at many levels of consciousness higher than the consciousness awareness we have in the physical realm. Nothing physical can break that connection of consciousness because it is inherently spiritual. The death of your loved one's physical body only breaks the connection of the outermost layer of ego-consciousness. While the connections at many higher levels of consciousness remain, the mutual love between you and your loved one remains.

Consciousness is not trapped by time and space

Time, space and consciousness are interrelated and create our four-dimensional physical world (i.e. length, breadth, height and time). Time, space, matter and gravity are physical-realm manifestations of consciousness. It is consciousness that underpins time, space, matter and gravity. In the spiritual realm, physical matter does not exist and there are greater distortions in linear time, space and gravity. At the highest level of soul-consciousness the concepts of time, space, matter and gravity do not apply because that level of consciousness is deathless, timeless, wholly unified and all-pervasive.

The past and the future are illusions created by the brain trapped by the concept of linear time

Linear time comprises a past, present and a future with each aspect following the other in a forward linear fashion. But time is 'rubbery', not like a rigid one-directional 'arrow'. Even many laws of physics can function perfectly well if linear time is reversed. The brain creates the illusion of one-directional linear time simply to make sense and order of reality. Although physical reality requires the linear flow of time, spiritual reality does not. At the highest levels of consciousness, there is no past and no future, no beginning and no end, no birth and no death – only conscious awareness of the eternal present. Consequently, the perception of time depends on the vibrational frequency of consciousness. Time is an entirely subjective experience. The higher your vibrational frequency, the slower the flow of linear time. At the highest vibrational frequencies of consciousness, linear time slows or 'stretches' to the point where the past and future dissolve into only the present moment. Therefore, the concept of death only applies to your loved one's physical body and to only one small aspect of their ego-consciousness. Your loved one's higher levels of consciousness do not die when their physical body dies. And, of course, neither will yours.

Thoughts are not hindered by time and space

Communicating through thoughts with your loved one in the spiritual realm is just as easy as communicating with them as if they were in the physical realm. The brain creates the four-dimensional physical reality by slowing and filtering consciousness. Written or spoken language requires the illusion of linear time because language is linear, and it must be for it to be coherent. But thoughts are not linear because they are constructs of consciousness only. It is perfectly understandable and normal for you to want to talk to your loved one silently or aloud (if aloud it would be prudent to do it alone so others do not question your sanity). Whether your loved one has a physical body or not is irrelevant for communication because the soul is omniscient and hears everything.

Love

Love is an inherent principle of the universe that death cannot destroy

Love inherently acknowledges the interconnectedness and the oneness of souls that cannot be broken when a physical body dies. Love is a universal law that mirrors the all-pervasive law of gravity. Love is a spiritual force that connects all beings in the same way that the invisible force of gravity binds planets into orbits around stars, and galaxies into orbits around black holes. Love is a union of consciousness, and consciousness is a unifying force like the law of gravity. The physical and spiritual realms exist like an endless timeless ocean of consciousness. The ocean of consciousness is wholly unified so the universe, both its physical and spiritual aspects, is essentially a spiritual ocean of love. All sentient beings are inherently spiritually connected, to varying degrees, because we all swim in that universal spiritual ocean of love. As sentient beings, we are all driven at multiple levels of consciousness to love and to be loved. Love, in all its light and dark shades, shapes your life, the life of galaxies and the life of the universe. As soul-consciousness is your and your loved one's inherent essence, your and your loved one's inherent nature is love.

Love is the face of the soul

Cohesion and adhesion are the inherent properties of consciousness in a similar way to how cohesion and adhesion are the inherent properties of water. Water naturally seeks seamless union as droplets, pools, lakes or even oceans. Likewise, the nature of consciousness is to always seek union through love with other equivalent levels of consciousness. At the physical level, ego-consciousness will seek union with an equivalent ego-consciousness while soul-consciousness will seek union with an equivalent soul-consciousness. And it is the same for the countless levels of consciousness in between. These unions at corresponding levels of consciousness can be imagined to be like the perfectly horizontal 'rungs' that connect, at corresponding points, the two long vertical strands in the double-helix twisted ladder structure of DNA. That multilevel union of consciousness is the basis of love. The nature of consciousness is to always seek union through love. In that sense, love is the face of the soul. So the corresponding levels of purer ego-consciousness above the physical level remain connected between you and your loved one. The strength of your relationship with your loved one reflects the multiple levels of consciousness that both of you share and connect on.

Love is unity and oneness – in life and after death

As it is when two individual water droplets merge cohesively and there is no possibility to identify the original two droplets in the larger merged droplet, it is the same with our love relationships and the consciousness each of us brings to those relationships (no matter what the type of relationship). When you and your loved one connected in a union of love, the shared unified consciousness between the two of you became greater than the individual droplets of consciousness that each of you brought to your relationship. It would be impossible to identify which 'droplet' of consciousness is yours and which is your loved one's. That love union of consciousness is a unity that exists in life and after the death of their physical body.

Love is a spiritual attraction of consciousness between you and your loved one

Love is the mutual attraction and unification between you and your loved one at one or more corresponding levels of consciousness simultaneously. Love is a deep emotional, and even deeper spiritual, connection between you and your loved one. The attraction can encompass all levels of consciousness from the outermost layer of ego-consciousness through to soul-consciousness. At the physical level, the outermost aspect of ego-consciousness is strongly influenced by emotions, whereas higher levels of consciousness are more strongly influenced by the universal soul. If you believe that your loved one is your 'soul mate', it is likely that both of you share unified consciousness at many levels above the outermost layer of ego-consciousness. In general, you will share consciousness on many more levels with your family members and romantic partner than with friends or acquaintances. As your loved one's ego-consciousness at the physical level is only one aspect of ego-consciousness, there remains many more higher and purer levels of their ego-consciousness that are unaffected by the death of their physical body.

It is deep love that fuels your deep grief

The deeper you love, the deeper will be your grief because the bond between you and your loved one manifests at multiple levels of consciousness. The disengagement of one or more corresponding levels of consciousness creates feelings of emptiness and sometimes a feeling that a part of yourself is somehow missing. The part of you that is missing is that small part of ego-consciousness you shared with your loved one at the physical level. So as you and your loved one share a love union of consciousness at much higher levels than that of the physical level, your grief will be deeper because your spiritual connection is deeper.

Losing the physical presence of someone does not mean you have lost the person or that they have lost you

You remain connected with your loved one even after their physical body dies because of the shared consciousness between the two of you. Those unions of love at the higher levels of consciousness may even become stronger after the outermost layer of ego-consciousness connection is broken, if the connection between the two of you reaches levels of consciousness of extremely high vibrational frequencies. If so, you may feel their presence around you at certain times, because either you have thought of them or your loved one has thought of you.

Your memories of your loved one keep you connected to them

When your thoughts fill with memories of your loved one, you connect with them at every level of consciousness that the two of you share in spiritual union. The more levels of consciousness on which the two of you are connected, the more memories will fill your thoughts and the greater emotional intensity those memories will evoke. As the spiritual connection between you and your loved one is through shared consciousness, and at multiple levels, when you remember them, they remember you too at higher levels of consciousness.

There are physical and spiritual aspects of love

As it is in life, the love between you and your loved one has many different aspects and stages. It is the same after the death of your loved one's physical body. Consider how over time (even if it was a relatively short period) the love between the two of you changed and deepened as greater trust and mutual understanding developed. So your relationship with your loved one does not end with the death of their physical body, it simply enters a new stage in which the spiritual aspect is deepened. How you define the new relationship is entirely up to you and your loved one. It will depend on the shared consciousness between the two of you and how strong the connection is.

The spiritual connection between you and your loved one defines the truth and reality of the unending love between the two of you

While strong and important, the love at the physical level between you and your loved one is a reflection of the deeper and stronger spiritual love between the two of you at higher levels of consciousness. It is the deeper, higher spiritual connection between the two of you that ultimately defines more truthfully your love union. Soul-consciousness is the highest form of spiritual love between you and your loved one. Soul-consciousness is not born and is not subject to death. Soul-consciousness existed before the physical universe was created.

Death

Death is merely a portal through which consciousness passes unhindered by the physical body

The death of the physical body gives consciousness the opportunity to enter the spiritual realm without any obstacles of perception. While the physical body is alive and functioning normally, the brain through the five senses filters consciousness from the spiritual realm to create the four-dimensional physical realm. If the brain did not do this, we would be unable to live a normal life in the physical realm. When the physical body and brain die, the impediments of perception are removed and we can perceive the spiritual realm more fully. The spiritual realm is closer to the true reality of the universe than the physical realm because of the greater clarity of conscious awareness that is achieved at higher levels of consciousness.

Life and death are merely two different states of consciousness

In life, your senses distract you from having full access to the spiritual realm. Life gives you full awareness of the physical realm while the death of the physical body gives full awareness of the spiritual realm. Death is really only a different state of consciousness but of a higher vibrational frequency compared to the consciousness in the physical realm. When the physical body dies, the senses shut down and we become fully aware of the spiritual realm. The lower levels of consciousness, closest to the physical realm, are influenced more by ego-consciousness, which shapes your personality and the outermost layer of ego-consciousness. Your life experiences are the scaffolding on which your outermost layer of ego-consciousness is built. At the highest level of consciousness there is no trace of ego influence because there is only a universal soul-consciousness.

The beginning of life marks our entry into the physical realm while death marks our entry into the spiritual realm

A physical body with physical sensory faculties is necessary to function in the physical realm, but spiritual bodies with spiritual sensory faculties (known also as light bodies because that is how they are typically perceived) are required for the spiritual realm. Each subsequent and higher level of consciousness requires a different spiritual body to function at that level. For most people, we can have full awareness of only one level of consciousness at any given time. While in a fully functioning physical body, your awareness of numerous spiritual bodies and indeed soul-consciousness is blocked by your five senses and all the intervening levels of consciousness. The death of the physical body gives you full awareness of your spiritual environment at a particular level of consciousness. At soul-consciousness, no type of body is required because it is a unique conscious awareness of the universe at all the lower levels of consciousness simultaneously. Each of us functions at the level of soul-consciousness because that is our inherent nature but we are simply not fully conscious of it.

Death marks the end of our physical journey but the beginning of our spiritual journey

Life is a journey in the physical realm shaped by the choices we make. Each choice we make creates a ripple effect in the fabric of consciousness that radiates to all levels of consciousness like the ripple effect created in a pond when a pebble breaks the water's surface. Therefore, during our physical journeys and following the death of the physical body, choices we make shape our journeys in the physical realm as well as in the spiritual realm. As in a pond, the ripple effect on the water's surface radiates out in concentric circles to the shore then returns towards the point where the pebble entered the water. The causal or karmic effect of our choices is merely the returning waves of consciousness from higher spiritual levels of consciousness. Each level of consciousness will generate its own return waves of consciousness. Therefore, our choices and the effect of our choices shape our soul's journey in both the physical and spiritual realms.

Life reveals ego-consciousness but death can reveal soul-consciousness

Entry to the physical realm requires a physical body and a physical body requires an individualized consciousness because each of us has a unique individual body. That individualized consciousness is the outermost layer of ego-consciousness and is the most individualized form of consciousness. It matures and develops through our physical sensory perceptions and life experiences. Therefore, the death of a physical body is an opportunity for many levels of consciousness to be distilled away, making it possible to become aware of soul-consciousness.

When its time arrives, death should not be feared but should be embraced

The beginning of life (when conscious awareness enlivens a physical body) and death are markers of the natural cycle of consciousness. All biological entities are subject to the cycle of life and death. All natural cycles should be accepted and embraced rather than feared. All of us will be touched by the hand of death at the end of our physical lives. Just as consciousness is transitioned at the time of entry into the physical realm from the spiritual realm, it is also transitioned at the time of death from the physical realm to the spiritual realm. The outermost layer of ego-consciousness envelops all the higher levels of consciousness at the beginning of a physical life and develops during that life. So the death of your loved one's physical body is merely a transition of their consciousness through the discarding of that outermost layer of ego-consciousness, and is not the end of their existence.

To understand the meaning of life, you must first understand the meaning of death

Understanding the meaning of death acknowledges the inherent spiritual nature of one's being. We are spiritual beings who inhabit a physical body to function in the physical realm. Understanding the spiritual nature of your and your loved one's existence should reframe your perception of physical life in a spiritual context. Ultimately, the purpose and meaning of life and the purpose and meaning of death are the same – to deepen your sense of the spiritual. That purpose and meaning become clearly apparent when your physical body dies, but it can also become apparent before that happens through life's other spiritual experiences like your experience of grief when a loved one's physical body dies.

Death is pregnant with spiritual potential

Because the death of the physical body is a transition of consciousness to become fully aware of the spiritual realm, the potential to fully realize your inherent spiritual nature exists by attaining levels of consciousness approaching soul-consciousness. Not even the most subtle form of the ego remains at the level of soul-consciousness. Soul-consciousness is the underlying fabric of both the physical and spiritual aspects of the universe. The level of spirituality we attain at the time of death is dependent upon our spiritual development in the physical realm and at all the higher more subtle levels of ego-consciousness.

The soul stands fearless in the face of death

At the highest level of consciousness, the soul is the deathless spiritual essence of one's being devoid of any trace of ego or a sense of an individual 'I'. Death and birth occur at many spiritual levels, just as they occur at this physical level. Birth and death only occur wherever an awareness of ego-consciousness exists. The cycle of transforming and distilling consciousness that occurs during every death at any level of consciousness is merely the process of returning consciousness to its core soul state. Even though at higher levels of consciousness the ego becomes more subtle, our awareness at higher levels becomes clearer and more expansive because many more dimensions of awareness can be apprehended. However, the deathless soul is the unchanging essence of your being and cannot be touched by the hand of death because it is beyond linear time and space. The soul is not born and cannot die. As the soul cannot die, it is in a sense fearless in the face of death.

We were spiritual beings before we were physical beings

As inherently spiritual beings, our physical journey is ultimately an unnatural state of existence. The physical body is like a wet suit, face mask, fins and breathing apparatus that a scuba diver wears to dive deep under water. That equipment is necessary for the diver to stay under water for long periods, but that is not the diver's natural environment nor their natural state of being. The physical body is like scuba diving equipment because it is necessary for living in the physical realm. It is only when we 'take off' the physical body at the time of death that we become aware of our natural spiritual environment and our natural spiritual state of being.

Soul connections are not severed with the death of the physical body

Being spiritual in nature, soul connections are not reliant on anything physical. Soul connections exist outside of time and space. This means that they have no beginning and no end. Consequently, soul connections are not subject to birth and death. Therefore, although the death of your loved one's physical body disconnects the outermost layer of ego-consciousness between the two of you, higher and deeper connections of consciousness exist outside the illusion of linear time.

Life is the in-breath and death merely the out-breath on the spirit's timeless journey

A spirit undergoes countless transitions of consciousness in the physical and spiritual realms. Soul-consciousness transitions from many spiritual levels to the outermost layer of ego-consciousness in the physical realm to begin a physical life. Ego-consciousness transitions from the physical realm to the spiritual realm to recommence a spiritual life. The journey of your loved one's spirit continues in the spiritual realm, as yours will when the time arrives for your physical body to die, whenever that may be. Therefore, a physical life can be seen as the spirit's in-breath, and a physical death merely its out-breath on its journey through countless levels of consciousness.

Death is an illusion

Ultimately, death is an illusion because linear time and our four-dimensional physical reality are illusions created by our brains. Yes, at this level of consciousness your loved one's physical body dies, so your grief and the emotional upheaval you are experiencing is absolutely real. And the need to cope and heal is absolutely necessary. But the highest level of consciousness is not subject to the physical phenomenon we refer to as death. Soul-consciousness is a timeless and deathless state of existence. Therefore, at the deepest and highest spiritual level, death is truly an illusion and not to be feared. To be truly free of fear is to be liberated from the illusion of death.

Grief

Love is the pleasure of souls and grief is the pain of love

The source of your love is your soul and the source of your grief is your love. A life lived fully is a life that fully expresses the pleasurable moments of love and the painful moments of grief. Just as you fully accept and express unconditionally the pleasure through the love for your loved one, you should also unconditionally accept and express your grief for them, painful though it is. Every tear you cry empties the well of your grief into the stream of your soul. And the stream of your soul rushes forth to merge in the deep lake of your love.

Embrace your grief and you embrace the deep spiritual aspect of yourself

Own your grief and embrace it because when you embrace your grief fully, you embrace the deep spiritual aspect of yourself. Express your grief in whatever way you want and whenever you want. Your grief is an opportunity to honor your love for your loved one. By fully expressing and accepting your grief you are honoring your loved one's physical life and expressing your love for them. And in doing so, you are honoring their spiritual life too because your thoughts of them, your reflections and your emotions will connect with their consciousness at higher spiritual levels. Even if life's circumstance hindered you from fully expressing your love for your loved one while their physical body was alive, harbor no regrets because that could evoke misplaced guilt. It is never too late to love deeply and it is never too late to grieve deeply.

It is deep underlying spiritual love that evokes your grief not death

Your grief does not emanate from knowledge of the death, or impending death, of your loved one's physical body. Yes, the death of your loved one's physical body does make you grieve but your grief is actually originally evoked by your underlying spiritual love at the level of the soul. The inherent nature of soul-consciousness is perfect union or love; so when you lose full awareness of soul-consciousness, that separation is when the grieving process actually begins but at a much higher level of consciousness. And at the soul level there is no beginning and no end because the soul is not trapped by linear time. At the soul level there is only perfect, eternal union – love. So it is separation from that higher and deepest eternal union of love that evokes the underlying grief at all lower levels of consciousness.

Your sense of loss creates a void that can be filled with the most precious memories

Shared memories and shared love are the bridges of consciousness that connect you with your loved one. Embrace those precious memories and any emotions that they evoke. Relive loving moments shared with your loved one and create new ones to express your love creatively and fully. Relive special days, events, perhaps places visited together, conversations, even any special times when you and your loved one simply shared each other's company in silence. Perhaps create a montage of photos or videos; write about your loved one whether privately or publicly; if you are musically inclined, consider composing music inspired by your memories of them. Be creative. Do anything that you feel will honor the memories of your loved one. In the spiritual realm, your loved one can create new memories of you too. Any new memories that either of you create will resonate at higher levels of consciousness and deepen the love between the two of you.

Your grieving heart reflects the love pangs of your soul

The power of grief comes from the power of love. The deeper you love someone while their physical body is alive, the deeper will be your grief when their physical body dies. A grieving aching heart reflects the love pangs of your soul. It is only through ego-consciousness that you experience grief because it creates a reality of individualism and separateness. The soul creates a unified reality where the concept of separation cannot exist so it cannot experience grief. Deepening your sense of the spiritual and raising your level of consciousness moves you closer to soul-consciousness. Consequently, with the changing of your perceptions and rising of your consciousness, you will experience less pain and more spiritual love. As inherently spiritual beings with the capacity for full awareness of soul-consciousness, our nature is to love. If we did not experience love, we would not experience grief.

The fragility and vulnerability that you feel are not weaknesses but strengths in the eyes of the soul

Acknowledging and embracing all the emotions that your grief evokes, including any feelings of fragility and vulnerability, is important for your well-being. Embracing your emotions while you grieve is an expression of love for yourself, your loved one and your soul. A sense of fragility and vulnerability has the potential to deepen your connection with your soul-consciousness because the experience opens you to deeper spiritual aspects of yourself. Hence, any feelings of fragility and vulnerability you may experience are actually strengths because they make you more receptive to the spiritual and more open to an awareness of soul-consciousness.

Your grief for your loved one is as personalized and unique as your love for them

Each of us is unique. We each have unique life experiences that shape our personalities and behaviors. Our uniqueness makes the loving relationships we have with others unique. The relationship with your loved one shapes the way you grieve for them because you will remember their unique mannerisms, like their habits, the way they looked into your eyes at special moments, the way they caressed you, slept, ate, walked, ran, spoke, sang, smiled, laughed, danced and cried. All those types of things uniquely define your loved one and your relationship with them. And those loving memories will define your grief. Talking to others willing to genuinely listen would be helpful, but recalling those memories in quiet reflection is just as beneficial and sometimes it is simply more convenient to do so.

Your grief is a natural process like the ebb and flow of moon tides rolling onto a beach

Your grief is normal and natural. Like the process of grief, the high and low moon tides are not destroyers of the beach but are gentle re-shapers and transformers of the coastline. Whether we become aware of it or not, grief changes whoever it touches and every one of us will be touched at some time in our lives. You can embrace the transformation and deepen your sense of the spiritual or deny it. Denying it only postpones the inevitable. Even if you do not embrace the transformation and accept that your sense of the spiritual can be deepened through the grieving process, you will be unable to avoid a profound transformation when your own physical body eventually dies and your consciousness transitions to the spiritual realm.

Grief and love are emotions experienced by all conscious beings and are not dependent on a physical body being alive

Your loved one feels the same grief and love that you do. It does not matter that their physical body may have already died. Your loved one's distilled and clarified ego-consciousness remains intact and harbors memories of you and their other loved ones from their physical life. At more subtle levels of ego-consciousness in the spiritual realm, your loved one can reflect on their physical life and their relationship with you. When they do, they make a spiritual reconnection with you. Therefore, your loved one's memories of you mean that they experience the same grief and love that you do.

Love is a dance between the head and the heart while grief is a dance between the heart and the soul

The rational mind and the emotional heart can sometimes appear to be in a dance within the context of a love relationship, especially in the beginning of that type of relationship. One day you move closer to your loved one under the influence of your heart then later, as if the music stops or the rhythm changes, you move away under the influence of your head. Just as love is like a dance, so is your grief. In your grief, that same type of dance prevails between your emotional heart and the soul essence of your being. Both the heart and the soul yearn for a union of love but in different realms – the heart in the physical realm and the soul in the spiritual realm. The soul knows that the death of the physical body draws consciousness closer to its spiritual home. However, your emotional heart yearns for your loved one's physical presence. Your heart and your loved one's heart yearn for the physical connection between the two of you. Yet your soul and your loved one's soul yearn for a spiritual union.

A sense of closure opens doors of resolution but it may never completely end the grieving process

The grieving process is not neat and linear with a beginning and end. Years may pass yet an anniversary of a special event, a memory, a song, a book, a movie, even the anonymous unconnected gaze of a stranger in the street who reminds you of your loved one can trigger moments of grief unexpectedly. The pain and feelings of confusion, emptiness, fragility and vulnerability can reemerge at any time. Accept grief as a lifelong friend that may come and go as it pleases. As with all friendships, over time your relationship with grief will change but the relationship will always remain to some degree.

Grief is a spiritual wound

Your grief is complex and multilayered. Grief is a wound of your spirit and that wound manifests psychologically even sometimes physically in the form of pain. Consequently, healing that wound requires a holistic approach that acknowledges your spiritual nature and the spiritual nature of your grief. Some spiritual practices may help heal your grief wound and can complement any mainstream psychological therapy you may feel is necessary. Try to be open-minded yet vigilant about different spiritual practices. You may never know if something is beneficial unless you actually try it. And learning something new and interesting can potentially bring you a new circle of friends and point your life's compass in a more positive direction. There are also various therapeutic modalities that acknowledge the spiritual aspect of our beings and these may also help the healing process because many have multilayered approaches. So think about finding and exploring different therapies and practices to heal your spirit. Healing your spirit will assist in healing your grief.

Your grief will test your faith in many things and some questions may remain unanswered

Many questions can arise while you grieve. You may ask yourself questions like: "Why are we born?", "Why do we die?", "Why am I here?", "What is the meaning of life?", "Is there life after death?", "Is there a God?", "What defines the concept of God?" Questions like these are the starting point for positive self-reflection or introspection. And self-reflection is the foundation stone for your spiritual journey. Answers to all your questions may not be found easily but it is not the answers that are important, it is the asking of the correct questions. If you ask the correct questions, you will obtain the appropriate answers in one form or another at the right time. It is through the correct questions that your sense of the spiritual will deepen and your transformative spiritual journey will begin.

A life lived with positive intentions is a life lived fully consciously

Grief provides an opportunity for you to ask questions about whether you feel you have sufficient purpose and meaning in your life to be completely satisfied and content. Are there goals you have always wanted to achieve but need to make deliberate decisions about to actually start achieving them? Are there places you have always wanted to visit? Long-lost friends with whom to reconnect? New skills to learn or knowledge to acquire? Compassionate causes to support? Through reflection on your life and your goals, you can consciously begin authoring the next chapter of your life while always remembering the previous chapters. A time of grief can be the beginning of a new chapter in the much larger book of your life, which could have positive implications for your journey in the spiritual realm too, whenever that journey is to begin.

Find peace in your grief

While you are grieving there may be times when you feel stressed and confused. Your grief may sometimes feel like you are completely alone and struggling to swim in a vast, cold, dark ocean. Believing that you must always be swimming can sometimes be the issue. You do not have to always be struggling. Floating is easy if you relax and simply stop struggling against the tide, and see the water not as your enemy but as your friend. Even if you cannot swim, each of us has the instinctive ability to float. Find moments of peace in your grief. Where you find silence, you will find peace. Create the physical and mental space to reflect in silence. Switch off all your mobile devices so you cannot be disturbed. It may help if you close your eyes, release any tension in your body and sit or lie comfortably. Breathe slowly and deeply. As your breathing slows, allow each inhale and exhale to be increasingly shallow until they become natural and normal. Peaceful silent moments can be found in a quiet part of your home, and equally in a forest, in a park, at a beach or a lake. Silence should not be feared or undervalued. If you fear silence, you really fear yourself because silence takes you closer to your deeper spiritual core. Entering silence takes you into the embrace of the soul. A deeper you, closer to the soul, will reveal a wiser you and give you access to higher levels of consciousness.

The uplifting wings of reflection reside in what can seem like the cold dark depths of grief

In the peace of silence, you have the opportunity to reflect. Reflection is an important part of learning about yourself, and more importantly about your inherent spiritual nature. Perhaps at the same time each day, allow yourself to create the mental space to simply pause and quietly reflect. Make whatever time you can in the day or night to quietly reflect on your relationship with your loved one, on your own life and the life that the two of you shared. Also think about what values you shared with your loved one. And how have those shared values shaped your personal core values and vice versa? How did your loved one's life change yours in positive ways and how did your life positively change theirs? One or two minutes may be all you can manage initially because some memories may evoke too much pain – that is under-standable. The important point is that you start the process. Through quiet introspection, you honor the unique relationship with your loved one and honor them. But it is also an opportunity for you to honor yourself and your own life.

Grief is like a hunger that can be fed with the food of reflection

Through silent reflection on the nature of consciousness, death, grief and love, your sense of the spiritual will deepen and your conscious awareness will heighten and widen to higher levels of consciousness like ever-widening concentric circles of light one on top of the other. As your sense of the spiritual deepens and your consciousness rises, your relationship with grief and how you perceive it will change. You may perceive yourself, the people around you and the world differently. Importantly, you may realize there is a spiritual reality beyond the physical reality where your loved one's journey continues. That spiritual reality lies within the peace of your reflective silence. For peace and silence are the wings of the soul.

Your grieving heart can be shrouded in the cold darkness of negativity or open to the warm light of transformation

As it is in all aspects of our lives, our choices define the trajectories of our journeys. It is your choice how you perceive your grief. If you perceive your grief only as a negative painful experience, the opportunity to transform your consciousness and deepen your spirituality will be impeded. Your grief is painful and the emotions you experience are strong. But it is possible to see your grief as more than only a painful negative experience. To see your grief as only a painful negative experience is to see only one-half of the grief and be blinded to the opportunity of spiritual transformation that resides in your grief. When you see grief holistically, you will see its light of transformation too.

Transformation

When you forgive yourself you see the source of love within you and you open the door of transformation

During your grief, there may be times when you experience a sense of guilt perhaps because of a certain aspect of your relationship with your loved one. Perhaps your guilt is triggered by something you said to your loved one or did, or perhaps did not say or do, and you understandably regret that. While any sense of guilt is a natural response to something you may regret, it is also a potential barrier to transformation. If your loved one was physically present, what would you say or do to deal with any sense of guilt you may feel? If you feel comfortable doing so, now is an opportunity to say or do whatever you want to express how you feel to your loved one. Remember, whenever you think of your loved one, you make a connection with them at higher levels of consciousness, so it does not matter if they are physically present or not. Say or do whatever you feel you must as often as you feel is necessary to forgive yourself. It can be difficult because most of us find it much easier to forgive others than to forgive ourselves. When you forgive others, you see the source of love within them, but when you forgive yourself you see the source of love within you. Once you see the source of love within you, you open the door of transformation.

Transformation begins within you and is impeded only by your perceptions and your choices

Acknowledging and accepting that death and grief present spiritual opportunities is a choice that you make. Your belief system is framed by your perceptions. And your perceptions are influenced by choices you make. The books you read, the entertainment you watch, the people you befriend are all as a result of choices you make. Changing your perceptions and the choices you make could change your life in positive ways. Questions are precursors to change. Questioning your perceptions is healthy because perceiving without questioning will prevent you from expanding your consciousness and making wise decisions informed by a spiritual awareness and higher levels of consciousness. A life without questions is a life without answers. And a life without even an inkling of any answers is a life lived in the darkness of ignorance.

Transformation is a journey of process not a race with a finish line

Embark on the journey of transformation in your own time and at your own pace. Deepening your sense of the spiritual will rarely occur through some sort of mystical epiphany, although this is certainly possible. In most cases, the journey begins with questions to yourself about life and death – what purpose do they serve? What meaning can be found in life and is there any meaning to be found in death? How can any meaning be found? What positive purpose and meaning does the death of your loved one's physical body serve, either for you personally or for others they knew, or for those who at least knew of them? You may ask such questions to those you trust and respect. You may be motivated to seek out information about spiritual matters through various sources. All the while, your sense of the spiritual will be slowly deepening as the spiritual aspects of life and death inevitably become more apparent. Over time, you may decide to make small but important changes to your lifestyle that reflect your rising and widening level of consciousness and your deepening sense of the spiritual. Any changes you make in the physical realm will influence your journey in the spiritual realm after the death of your physical body, whenever that will be. So your journey of transformation will not end when your physical life ends. It is a journey that will continue as long as your full awareness of soul-consciousness is unattained.

Within your greatest fears resides the opportunity to evoke your strongest courage

Like deep love, death and grief awaken the spirit and stir the soul. No one can be unmoved when in love or when we face the death of a loved one's physical body. Following a death, the transformation can be deeper than the transformative effect of emotions evoked by a love relationship within the physical realm because of the spiritual forces involved. Therefore, a time of grief is an opportunity to transform relationships, careers, and your perceptions in positive and profound ways. You may question whether you are living your life in a way that is consistent with your personal core values, and whether you are being the best person you can be for yourself and those around you. The profundity of the spiritual transformation may create fear in you because the potential changes you can make in your life can be far reaching. But your strongest courage and highest potential can be realized from unexpected situations and from within your greatest fears.

Transformation begins with acceptance of yourself, your grief, the death of the physical body, and the deathless soul

If you are unable to fully accept your grief, no matter what form your grief may take, you will be unable to use the experience to make positive changes within yourself. Your grief is a natural process just as the death of the physical body is a natural process. As are the love between you and your loved one, the shared consciousness between you and your loved one, and the journey of the deathless soul. All these processes are interconnected, nonlinear and cyclical, meaning that one process can merge into another and each effectively has no beginning and no end. If you view death, grief, consciousness and love in a spiritual context you will be open to a deepening sense of the spiritual that will inevitably transform your perceptions of yourself and how you perceive the world.

An open mind is a mind always open to the mysteries of the universe

If the shiniest and largest of mirrors is always kept in a dark room, it will never reflect any light. To transform your thinking you will need to be open to the positive light of spirituality and not trapped by a mind that may be closed to even the possibility of higher levels of consciousness beyond the physical realm. The physical realm is only one small aspect of the universe. An open mind is the doorway to new possibilities of perceiving yourself and the universe quite differently. Entering through that doorway, the light of your mind can reach deeper within yourself and far into the spiritual universe. And the more the mirror of your mind is turned towards the light, the more light it will reflect and the deeper that light will penetrate the mysteries of the universe.

Deep reflection allows more light into the mirror of your mind

When you take time to quietly reflect, you open up the possibility of new ways to perceive and new ways to think about life, death, grief and love. A quiet, still, reflective and open mind cannot be held captive in the physical realm and it has unfettered access to all spiritual dimensions. The deeper within yourself you delve, the higher your consciousness will rise like increasingly higher and widening circles of light. Elevating your consciousness will allow you to have a more positive outlook on your life and the lives of those around you.

Transformation is an opportunity to bring more light, love, healing and spirituality into your life

A transformation of consciousness allows you access to higher levels of consciousness and to deepen your sense of the spiritual. As your sense of spirituality deepens, doors leading to higher levels of consciousness and more profound transformations will present themselves to you, perhaps in the most surprising and mysterious ways. It is your choice to open those doors when you are ready to do so. Do not close doors of transformation before they have a chance to open. The doors of transformation bring more light, love, healing and spirituality into your life. And a transformed life will inevitably result in a transformed death.

The soul is like a fragile seed requiring the rich soil of silence, the pristine rain of reflection, the warm light of love and an open heart of humility

Increasingly subtle forms of ego-consciousness are subjected to the cycle of birth and death within the physical and spiritual realms of consciousness. Each birth and death is transformative and profound in their own way, relative to the particular level of consciousness. At each progressively higher level of consciousness, your conscious awareness heightens and widens, and awareness of your soul essence deepens. But the most profound transformative transition of consciousness occurs when awareness of soul-consciousness is attained. Through regular periods of deep silence, reflection, love and humility your perceptions change. And your thinking changes. Your life will change. If your life changes, your death will change too because you will realize that death has profound spiritual potential. And if you see death as a transformative event then you must also see that your grief has the potential to transform you too.

Silence, reflection, love and humility are the most precious offerings on the sacred altar of the soul

Soul-consciousness is the consciousness of the universe, encompassing both the physical and spiritual realms. It is the antithesis of the outermost layer of ego-consciousness that thrives on physical stimuli through the senses. Entering a deep peace and silence and quietly reflecting on your grief with a mindset of humility is an effective way of stopping physical stimuli feeding the ego. When the ego is starved, your soul is nourished and your sense of the spiritual is deepened. As soul-consciousness unifies the entire universe, it is the highest and purest form of love. Therefore, silence, reflection, love and humility can assist you to move closer to an awareness of soul-consciousness and further away from the raw pain of grief.

Silence is not a void, it is overflowing with spirituality

A peaceful, quiet mind embraces silence. Silence does not equate with emptiness. Silence is filled with positive spiritual opportunities. Silence is the path that takes you to deeper levels of spirituality and higher levels of consciousness. Do not be afraid of silence because within silence and at higher levels of consciousness you will find a more authentic and spiritual you. Only when you are silent can you listen to the voice of your spiritual essence – the mysterious harmony of the universe or the 'music of the spheres'. That is the sound of your soul. When you lovingly embrace silence, you lovingly embrace yourself and the entire universe simultaneously. The deeper you go into silence, the deeper you go into yourself and the further you go into the universe.

Death is an opportunity to transform consciousness for the dying while grief is an opportunity to transform consciousness for the living

When your loved one's physical body dies, it is transformative because their perceptions will be changed from an awareness of only a physical reality to an awareness of a spiritual reality. As you grieve, you can also be transformed in a similar way by acknowledging and accepting that the death of your loved one's physical body is an event with spiritual implications. And deepening your sense of the spiritual will transform the way you perceive your grief, life, death, love, and even yourself.

Grief, like death, is a spiritual journey of transformation

Beyond the distress, confusion, emptiness and pain of grief, you may one day see the death of your loved one's physical body and your grief as precious gifts. In the final analysis, both death and grief are journeys into the spiritual. One is a journey for your loved one and the other a journey for you. Both death and grief inevitably lead to an exploration of consciousness, life and love, the result of which can be profoundly transformative. Perceiving death as a transition of consciousness with profound spiritual implications may positively alter your experience of grief and how you perceive life. For in finding the spiritual purpose and meaning of death and grief, you will find the spiritual purpose and meaning of life and love.

Afterword

Grief is a normal emotional response to death, or the imminent death, of your loved one's physical body or perhaps the impending death of your own body. Your views of death frame your views on grief. Accepting that death has a profound spiritual aspect can ease the pain and emotional upheaval of grief because it places death in a much broader context. The process of grief is essentially a spiritual opportunity in the same way that death is a spiritual opportunity. Grief is, as is death, an exploration of consciousness and a journey of the spirit. In both cases, your guide and teacher on that journey is your soul. As the nature of the soul is love, your grief is not only a manifestation of a deep love for your loved one but it is also a clarion call to you from your spiritual core. So when you fully embrace your grief, you embrace your own spiritual essence and the opportunity for spiritual transformation.

The death of the physical body does not extinguish consciousness. Death only transitions and distils consciousness from the physical body to the spiritual realm. This is not merely wishful thinking. The mountain of literature on near-death experiences provides significant evidence from thousands of people from around the world and different religious (and nonreligious) backgrounds indicating that consciousness can and does exist independently of the physical body. This evidence is supported by the firsthand experiences of many in the medical profession and by the findings of scientific studies.

Consequently, grief deserves to be perceived holistically within a spiritual context, in the same way that consciousness, death, love and transformation deserve to be. The grief you feel is the same grief that your loved one feels even after their physical body dies. Your grief is shared with your loved one just as the love between both of you continues to be shared at higher levels of consciousness. Their soul's journey continues in the spiritual realm, while for now your soul's journey continues in the physical realm.

We experience a physical death because we experience a physical life. And we experience grief because we experience love. Love is the inherent and instinctive nature of consciousness. All conscious beings are driven to love and to be loved. To be conscious is to seek love – consciously and unconsciously – because the pursuit of love or unification plays out at all higher levels of consciousness simultaneously. Spirituality is the basis of love, life, death and grief. Each of those experiences presents opportunities for you to transform spiritually. You simply need to be open to such a positive transformation. Embracing those experiences can begin with silent reflection on your perceptions of the nature of consciousness, death, grief, love and transformation. In doing so, you create the opportunity to deepen your sense of the spiritual, and rediscover your inherent nature.

The soul stands fearless in the face of death. You now have an opportunity to stand fearless, reflective and resilient in the face of the physical life ahead of you. Just as your loved one has the opportunity to reflect on their physical life lived after their physical body dies, you have the opportunity to reflect on your physical life to live in the context of your grief. Your life can be lived ignoring your inherent spirituality or you can fully accept and embrace it. By embracing your spirituality, you embrace your grief, death, life and love – love for your loved one and love for your soul. So if you deeply embrace your inherent spirituality, you become receptive to a deep transformation that can realign the compass and trajectory of your life, not just in the physical realm but in the spiritual realm too.

Take comfort knowing that the death of your loved one's physical body is merely the conclusion of a single chapter in the endless book of their soul's journey. The complex and rich story of their soul's journey continues, at higher more subtle levels of consciousness, to be authored by them. Your soul's journey continues to be authored by you. For you, the grieving process can be the beginning of a new transformative chapter in the endless book of your soul's story. You now have an opportunity to write that story with a deepened spiritual conviction. That conviction could prove to be prudent preparation for your own journey of profound transformation into the spiritual realm, whenever that special door opens for you.

If you are experiencing ongoing severe psychological issues because of the death of a loved one's physical body, please consider contacting a mental health professional or seeking advice from a grief support group.

B O O K S

O is a symbol of the world, of oneness and unity; this eye represents knowledge and insight. We publish titles on general spirituality and living a spiritual life. We aim to inform and help you on your own journey in this life.

Visit our website: http://www.o-books.com

Find us on Facebook:
https://www.facebook.com/OBooks

Follow us on Twitter: @obooks